THAT SILVER SHORE
EASTER MUSICAL WITH TEN SONGS

An old farmer bargains with the Angel of Life in this parable of Springtime and New Life.

The farmer was out walking in the woods one day when he was visited by the Angel of Life who told him that it was time to put his business in order and to leave this world for the next. He was devastated and cried out, "But I have just married a young wife, I cannot leave her – just like that."

The angel told him that there was only a fixed amount of lifetime in the world at any one moment and the old farmer had run out of his allotted time. But if the farmer could find someone to give or sell him some of their lifetime, the Angel of Life could accept such a bargain. The angel gave him a short while to find someone otherwise the farmer would have to leave this world. The farmer was at his wits end.

The situations, characters and songs that follow tell the story of the farmer's progress.

LIFE OF DREW CARSON

Sam Drew Carson was born in the North of Ireland and educated there at Wellington College and the Ulster Polytechnic. He completed his education in the USA at New Mexico Highlands University and the University of Arkansas and has traveled widely in North America, around the Atlantic and in Europe.

Drew worked as a seaman and fish-gutter in Vestmannaeyjar off the coast of Iceland. He lived and worked in the Irish and Western Isles Gaeltachts and was married in Welsh-speaking Carmarthen after which he honeymooned in Belfast. He has told his stories, composed and sung his songs, seeking storylines in Bristol and the English Westcountry. Drew has also lived and written in Nashville, Tennessee, in the wooded hills of Mid-America and from the Appalachians to the Ozarks. This was the culture that gave rise to the now worldwide Scotch-Irish country music.

In the USA, he also worked beside the bayous of the French-speaking Cajuns in the South and among the Western Spanish-speaking Navajos, Apaches and Pueblos of the Sangre de Cristo Mountains in New Mexico.

Drew has sailed far into the seas of old Gaelic and Oriental legend. After many years searching for inspiration for story and music, the author is still traveling and writing.

BOOKS BY THE SAME AUTHOR

ZENISUB –
Fun and Games in Businezz
ISBN: 978-0-9561435-2-5

GOOD FOR A LAUGH –
Six Funny Playscripts for Amateurs
ISBN: 978-0-9561435-3-2

HOME WITH A GOOD COMPANION –
Amateur Pantomime Scripts for a Merry Winter
ISBN: 978-0-9561435-4-9

CLASSIC EUROPEAN LYRICS –
Translated from the Gaelic, the French and Spanish
ISBN: 978-0-9561435-6-3

COMMONWEALTH –
An Introduction to Business Economics
ISBN: 978-0-9561435-7-0

MISSING PERSONS –
Detective Felix O'Neill in a Crime Adventure
ISBN: 978-0-9561435-8-7

WEREWOLF MURDERS –
Detective Felix O'Neill in a Crime Adventure
ISBN: 978-0-9561435-9-4

ORIENTAL GOVERNESS –
Detective Felix O'Neill in a Crime Adventure
ISBN: 978-1-908184-00-9

EASTER AND THE SPRINGTIME
Five Amateur Playscripts of New Life
ISBN: 978-1-908184-02-3

WALLWAVE THE SEA WARRIOR
Adventures of War Queens and Battle Heroes
ISBN: 978-1-908184-03-0

WALLWAVE THE SEA PRINCE
Adventures of War Queens and Battle Heroes
ISBN: 978-1-908184-04-7

WALLWAVE THE SEA KING
Adventures of War Queens and Battle Heroes
ISBN: 978-1-908184-05-4

THAT SILVER SHORE
Easter Musical with Ten Songs
ISBN: 978-1-908184-06-1

That Silver Shore

Easter Musical with Ten Songs

DREW CARSON

Order from:
https://www.createspace.com/4127009

Legals

ISBN: 978-1-908184-06-1

CONTENTS

THAT SILVER SHORE
Easter Musical with Ten Songs

ABOUT THE PLAY

An old farmer was out walking in the woods one day when he was visited by the Angel of Life. The angel told him that it was time to put his business in order and to leave this world for the next. The farmer was devastated and cried out, "But I have just married a young wife, I cannot leave her – just like that."

The angel told him that there was only a fixed amount of lifetime in the world at any one time. The old farmer had run out of his allotted lifetime. Of course, if someone sold or gave the farmer any of their time then he could use that extra time until it ran out. The angel gave the farmer a short while to make a bargain with someone.

The farmer was at his wits end. First, he went to his old friend Richman who could not be tempted by any amount of money.

The angel advised the farmer to try a poorman but Poorman also refused the offer saying, "I'd rather be poor than dead for the next five years or two years or whatever."

The old farmer began to think over his past life and the people he had known – even the shady characters. He visited a down-and-out hobo den and asked the hobos if they would sell him some of their time to lengthen his life.

Two old friends, a man and a woman, had become separated by the wars that were always being waged around them. The reunited sweethearts were grateful to the old farmer for bringing them together again but they would not sell any of their newfound goodtime together.

After the farmer had asked and been denied by richman, poorman, beggarman and thief, he had to surrender to the Angel of Life. "I am now ready to go but my dear young wife will be so devastated and lost without me. Let me just bid her one last farewell."

The angel gave him the time he needed.

The old farmer did so but his wife wept and said, "But why didn't you ask me? I will gladly give you 20 years of my life so that we can both die in about 20 years time. I did not marry you just to become a widow rightaway. Ask the angel if this is acceptable."

The Angel of Life agreed joyfully, "It gives me no pleasure to do my sad duty and balance out the years unevenly. There are children who die too soon and old folk who die long after they can help anyone. That is the purpose of life – to help each other. This is why I gave you a chance to balance out the years for you are still active and can look after your farm and grow good food for many years to come."

So the old farmer and his young wife were spared from the ordeal of death and widowhood and they lived happily for about 20 more years.

The Playscript

OUTLINE OF THE PLAY

ACT ONE – THE ANGEL OF LIFE
Scene One: Out on the Farm
ACT TWO – RICHMAN, POORMAN
Scene One: A Neighbor Visits the Farm
ACT THREE – BEGGARMAN, THIEF
Scene One: A Tramp in a Hobo Den
Scene Two: Later in the Den
ACT FOUR – OLD FRIENDS
Scene One: Back at the Farm
Scene Two: Old Loves Revived - Finale
PLACE: Deep in the tree-covered hills, far away.
TIME: Long ago.
ACTION: Takes place during the course of a day from early morning until evening.

PRODUCTION NOTES

ACTORS:
Seven - 4 female, 3 male.
A troop of 3 - 7 singers and dancers.
AGE GROUPS: All.
STAGE TIME: About 2 hours.
SET: One set in two subsets.
OPTIONAL EXTRAS: Marching soldiers in any uniform of choice to march across stage in Act Three, Scene Two. Painted scenery or a big screen T.V. with video may be substituted.
SEASON: Early Springtime.

MUSIC - Ten songs:
Song of the Trees, *p. 14*
The Calling Angel's Song, *p. 18*
When Old Friends Meet, *p. 28*
The City's Toils and Snares, *p. 38*
Lady of Days Gone By, *p. 42*
The Calm Springtime Snow, *p. 44*
Does Pain Remain, *p. 48*
Sweethearts Lost in War, *p. 59*
Friends of Long Ago, *p. 69*
The Flying Song, *p. 71*

LIST OF CHARACTERS
DONALD - A Farmer
THE ANGEL OF LIFE
RICHARD - A Wealthy Farmer
JACK - A Hobo
LORITA - A Widow and Beggarwoman
ROSALEEN - Her Daughter, a Thief
MARCELLA - The Farmer's Wife
Three to twelve dancers as angels or (later) as
Queens of Spring. Singers.

ACT ONE
THE ANGEL OF LIFE

SCENE ONE: OUT ON THE FARM

*Somewhere in the far wooded back hills. The **curtain rises on Marcella**, the farmer's wife, a young woman, who is walking in the woods near a small farmhouse in the background. Hills and trees are also in the background. It is early spring and light snow is lingering here and there.*

Front-stage there are bushes, trees and scrub. Symbolic decorations may include springs, wells, creeks, trees, hogs, birds, squirrels, sheep, deer or turkey.

Right and center-stage, at present unlit and hidden by bushes, is an old overgrown graveyard now used as a hobo den by down and outs. This will be highlighted later.

*Marcella Sings*** SONG OF THE TREES
Sung: Slowly

VERSE ONE:

d   d   r   m   r   m   l   s-m   r   d l_1

I love to walk the woods and listen to the trees

  d   m-f   s   l   s m   d   m   *r*

Their music sings as seasons come and go

  d   d   r   m   r m-l   s-m   r   d l_1

These woods make songs as many colored as the trees

  d   d   r   m f   m   r   d   r   *d*

Some fast and laughing, some wind-wept and slow

  s   l-t d^1 t   t   l   s-l   s-m   d

The summer-song of trees is happy swinging blooms

  s   l   t d^1 t   t-l   s   m   r

A thousand leaves and rhythms all in one

  s   s   s m^1 r^1 r^1 d^1 l d^1 s   m   d

Bees hum and strum and birds like banjoes pick and peck

  d-d   r-m   f   m   r   d-r   d

Driven along by that old drummer sun

VERSE ONE:

I love to walk the woods and listen to the trees
Their music sings as seasons come and go
These woods make songs as many colored as the trees
Some fast and laughing, some wind-wept and slow
The summer-song of trees is happy swinging blooms
A thousand leaves and rhythms all in one
Bees hum and strum and birds like banjoes pick and peck
Driven along by that old drummer sun.

VERSE TWO:
Then violins of autumn play across the woods
And far sad songs sweep out the falling leaves
Leaves blow up high and scatter and turn round and cry
That is the fall-song of the dying trees
And winter woods play long horn in a low cold march
A drum beats dim and darkly far from home
A ballad wails of travelers desperate and lost
The winter-song of woods that weep alone.

VERSE THREE:
Then spring woods sing and ring with light and fairy flutes
They play the lively tunes of old-time dance
As birds and squirrels jump the trees and drink the rain
The spring-woods swing the music of romance
Spring after winter, good times after not so good
Great songs revived, like happy days recalled
Old loves re-flamed long after sadness and defeat
This is the spring-song trees sing best of all.

MARCELLA: *(thinking aloud)* Why am I singing with such expectancy? Perhaps an important guest is coming. I can almost sense a strange presence today. Someone important must be coming to visit us. How exciting! I wonder if they'll bring good news or bad? But why am I saying such a superstitious thing? Yet I do feel uneasy.

Enter Donald. He is a heroic figure dressed as a prosperous farmer. He is of a mature age and considerably older than his wife.

MARCELLA: Ah, Donald my dear, I've just been walking in the woods. I'll go back now and do some work with the horses. Are you coming?

DONALD: *(appears tired)* No I'll join you later Marcella.

MARCELLA: Well if you wish to come and join me I'll be at the paddock.

DONALD: My dear I feel a little tired today, I don't know why. But I'll rest for a while here under the old oak and join you later. *(he sits down)*

MARCELLA: Take it easy.

*She sings Verse Three of **SONG OF THE TREES** again.*

VERSE THREE:
Then spring woods sing and ring with light and fairy flutes
They play the lively tunes of old-time dance
As birds and squirrels jump the trees and drink the rain
The spring-woods swing the music of romance
Spring after winter, good times after not so good
Great songs revived, like happy days recalled
Old loves re-flamed long after sadness and defeat
This is the spring-song trees sing best of all.

Marcella kisses Donald on the cheek **then she leaves stage left**. *Donald relaxes under the old oak.*

Enter from right-stage the Angel of Life followed by three to twelve angels.

The angels are veiled in white and dressed in traditional-style white angelic dresses. The Angel of Life is also dressed in white but is taller and more imposing than the others.

They all dance around the set and join in singing together:

THE CALLING ANGEL'S SONG –
ALONG THAT SILVER SHORE
Sung: Sweetly and Plaintively

VERSE ONE:

d - d   f   d   f - s   l   l   taw taw - taw   d^l
 O   come where song birds sing and all the wild woods

taw l taw l f s
are   ringing

d^l - taw   l - l   l -f s
Where fragrant flowers sway

d^l - taw   l   f   f - s   l - s
 O   come, O come away

d - d   f   s   l   taw - l   s   f - m f
Where slow songs glide along that silver shore

REFRAIN:

  s   l   s   m   d   d - r   m
Blow, blow, so free the breezes flow

d   d   s$_1$ d   r   m   m   f   s   r
To soothe the eyes with airs so soft and low

s - s   s   s - s - s   m   f
Over there is a light of dawn

  s   f - m   d   d - r - m   r
With a flame that lingers on

s$_1$ - s$_1$ d   r - m f - r   r   d t$_1$ d
Dreams come alive along that silver shore

VERSE ONE:
O come where song birds sing
And all the wild woods are ringing
Where fragrant flowers sway
O come, O come away
Where slow songs glide along that silver shore.

REFRAIN:
Blow, blow, so free the breezes flow
To soothe the eyes with airs so soft and low
Over there is a light of dawn
With a flame that lingers on
Dreams come alive along that silver shore.

VERSE TWO:
O hear the streamlets sigh
And the waterfalls a-crying
There the dark-red honeys glow
And the sweetening vinelets grow
For wines are deep along that silver shore.

REFRAIN:
Blow, blow, so free the breezes flow
To soothe the eyes with airs so soft and low
Over there is a light of dawn
With a flame that lingers on
Dreams come alive along that silver shore.

The angels dance around Donald as he stands up and walks about somewhat drowsily. They move forward towards him, beckoning to him and calling softly "Come, come away." They retreat into the background, still beckoning but the Angel of Life remains and stands facing Donald, looking solemnly at him and still beckoning as the angels finish singing the **CALLING ANGEL'S SONG.**

ANGEL OF LIFE:
Brave man, you walk alone I see
You walk in dangerous company

Come Donald, your time on earth is over. The Great Master has sent me to call you. It is time for you to come home to the Hills of Everlasting Tomorrows.

DONALD: *(clutching his shoulder)* What was that stab of pain? Who are you? Who are these dancers? Who are you to tell me that I must die?

ANGEL OF LIFE: I am no one and nothing in myself but I have been sent by the Great Master of Life to bring you this forewarning. In this you are privileged as few have been, for you have been dutiful and hard-working. I am the Angel of Life.

These angels are my friends of springtime who will help to bear your sad soul, heavy with the sorrow of parting to the Spring Woods of Tomorrow. But you need not fear nor be sorrowful.

DONALD: *(in pain)* Indeed, I've heard it said that at the time of death strange events and apparitions occur.

ANGEL OF LIFE: These appearances have been known to some.

DONALD: *(resigned and solemn)* So you have come to forewarn me to make myself ready. How much time do I have left?

ANGEL OF LIFE: When the Great Master of Life calls, one must come. But he is not concerned with a few hours more or less, a half-day or a day perhaps. Your leaving is, how shall I put it, imminent.

I have no control over the giving of life. But it is good for you that I have come to warn you. For the Great Master has told me that you may make a deal with anyone to take over a part of that person's lifetime.

This is a special privilege to extend your days, Donald.

DONALD: Do you mean that you could take life away from one and give it to another?

ANGEL OF LIFE: No. It would be for you Donald to make a deal with someone. If that person will give or sell a part of his or her life to you, I can agree to that. Sometimes a poor person will sell a year or two of his allotted time to better enjoy the years left to him. The question is - Would a person rather live five years in wealth or six years in poverty? However, almost no one ever has a chance to buy or sell. Death usually comes inexorably.

DONALD: But why would such a thing be possible, for me to escape and buy someone else's lifetime?

ANGEL OF LIFE: The Great Master himself gave of his own life for others, to live among men and teach them that they might live better lives. He has given to each man and woman an allotted time. Yet sometimes he is moved to avoid injustice or unfairness and will allow a person to give or take of life vicariously.

DONALD: Then does this ever happen? This selling - this exchange.

ANGEL OF LIFE: It has been known, but rarely.

DONALD: *(humbly)* What do I have to exchange? I have a good farm but I must leave that to my young wife to provide a living for her after I am gone. Of course, I have some money saved.

ANGEL OF LIFE: Then I will give you twelve hours to beg, borrow or buy a few more years but at the end of this period your time will be finished if you have made no agreement.

DONALD: *(shaking his head)* This is all like a bad dream.

ANGEL OF LIFE: I warn you that it will not be easy to find anyone who will sell you a few more years of life. Really, it would be better if you could resign yourself to crossing over to the other side. We have come to take you to a better place. Fruitful hills beyond. There will be no more regrets on the other side and you will be at peace.

DONALD: *(doubtful and troubled)* Perhaps I should resign myself to going. So let me die gracefully. First, let me bid farewell to my wife and neighbors like one who is going to a better land.

Donald joins the angels in singing the refrain of **THE CALLING ANGEL'S SONG** *as the angels and the Angel of Life continue to dance around Donald, beckoning and signaling "come away, come away."*

REFRAIN:
Blow, blow, so free the breezes flow
To soothe the eyes with airs so soft and low
Over there is a light of dawn
With a flame that lingers on
Dreams come alive along that silver shore.

ANGEL OF LIFE: If you are ready to come across the river with us now, let us go.

DONALD: *(in a quandary)* No, not yet. Let me think. Must I leave my farm and go to a land where things are not the same.

ANGEL OF LIFE: Just so.

DONALD: Oh let me think about that strange land for just a moment. *(he walks up and down)* I fear that I can't bear to leave this lovely world behind without a thought. Later perhaps but not now. I'm afraid. No. Give me the twelve hours you offered me to beg, borrow or buy a few more years.

ANGEL OF LIFE: But from whom? A richman, poorman, beggarman or thief? Life is life to everyone, no matter who they are. But . . very well, I will come with you to make quite sure that any deal you may make is fair and real. I will not be intrusive. Only those who need to will be able to see me. I will know if the giver has years to give and really means to give them.

DONALD: *(more optimistically)* Some of my oldest friends were killed or lost in the wars but I'll look for others who may wish to help me.

*The Angel of Life, the chorus of angels and Donald sing the second half of Verse 3 of **SONG OF THE TREES***

Spring after winter, good times after not so good
Great songs revived, like happy days recalled
Old loves re-flamed long after sadness and defeat
This is the spring-song, trees sing best of all.

All leave the stage, right.

- Curtain -

ACT TWO
RICHMAN, POORMAN

SCENE ONE:
A NEIGHBOR VISITS THE FARM

A neighbor visits the farm. Left and center-stage is still lit and right-stage is still in darkness. The scene is the same with optional minor variations such as the rearrangement of hogs, birds, squirrels, sheep, deer or turkey.

Enter Richard from left-stage. *He is a wealthy farmer.* ***Enter from right-stage the Angel of Life, unseen by Richard.*** *Choral singing and dancing by the angels includes bowing and shaking hands with each other.*

THAT SILVER SHORE

Donald sings

WHEN OLD FRIENDS MEET
Sung: Slowly with Feeling

> **VERSE ONE:**
>   d   m   m-m   r   m   s   s
> When old friends meet and greet, ah then
> d^1 l   s   l d^1 l   s-s
> The old bread springs to joyful grain
>   d-d   m   m m-r   m   s   *l*
> And the wine is always strong and sweet
>   s-s   m   r   d-d
> When old friends greet and meet
>   s-s d^1 d^1-t   t   l   l
> Good days will always fleet and flee
> d^1 s   l-l-s   f-m   m r-r
> And old times change with memory
>   d-d-m   m   m   r   m   s   *l*
> But old friends are real and whole and true
>   s - s   m   r   d-d
> When old friends meet anew
> d-r   m   r   d
> Old friends are few
>   d   r   m   m-m-r   *d*
> (So) Old friends are always new.

VERSE ONE:
When old friends meet and greet, ah then
The old bread springs to joyful grain
And the wine is always strong and sweet
When old friends greet and meet
Good days will always fleet and flee
And old times change with memory
But old friends are real and whole and true
When old friends meet anew
Old friends are few - (So)
Old friends are always new.

VERSE TWO:
Old hands are warm to grip and greet
And hearts will give a stronger beat
Dim eyes will see more clearly then
When old friends meet again
Good days will always fleet and flee
And old times change in memory
But old friends are real and whole and true
When old friends meet anew
Old friends are few - (So)
Old friends are always new.

DONALD: Richard, welcome to our farm.

RICHARD: How are you, Donald?

DONALD: Sit down Richard. I'm quite surprised to see you just at the time when I wanted to talk to you.

They sit on a fallen tree trunk. The Angel of Life lurks nearby, still unseen by Richard.

RICHARD: Right. It's all very strange, even uncanny in a way but I was dozing on the porch a little while ago and I had some kind of disturbing dream about you. I'm not sure what exactly it was but it was about some kind of danger you were in. It was like you were being chased or hunted or . . . *(he hesitates)*

DONALD: Or?

RICHARD: But it's so silly. You're looking so fine and fit and healthy.

DONALD: But what did you dream?

RICHARD: *(evasively)* I don't remember the details but it was something like . . as though someone was trying to take away your life. Who? Where? Why? I don't know, it was just something like that. But now I see that it was so nonsensical and pointless. It must be telepathy. You had some deep need and were on your way over to see your neighbor, eh? Right?

DONALD: Richard, your dream was truer than you realize. My life indeed is in great danger.

Donald looks at the Angel of Life who looks away.

RICHARD: Your life, surely not. Why, we're armed to the teeth around here . . . Count on us to defend you!

DONALD: No, the enemy isn't bandits or thieves. It sounds like just plain madness but the occasional pain in my back and shoulder has been so bad at times, bad enough for me to know I'm not dreaming. I know it's real, Richard. I'm in danger of dying . . . I really am.

RICHARD: Sure, Donald. I know you're not imagining it . . . You need a doctor.

DONALD: I'm afraid it's worse than that, Richard. I have been warned that my time is up.

RICHARD: So who warned you? Who threatened you and what was the meaning of my strange dream about you Donald?

DONALD: It sounds very strange but the Angel of Life has visited me and warned me that I must die or find someone to sell me some of their lifetime.

RICHARD: Someone to die earlier in your place but that's ridiculous, Donald. Really, this is going too far. You must have allowed a dream to upset your mind.

DONALD: I need to find someone to give me some of his or her years . . to substitute some of their lifetime for mine.

RICHARD: But Donald, surely that's impossible . . one person giving his or her life for another person. Why, it's just unnatural.

DONALD: Why so? Why should it not be possible? Do we really understand the force of life in the whole universe?

RICHARD: *(solemnly)* Well, it may be possible but it's just weird. You need to talk to some wise person about this. Logically, it sounds like it may be possible but it is terribly mystical and unusual.

DONALD: But let's just suppose for a moment that it is true.

RICHARD: *(condescendingly)* Yes, let's think about that now, logically Donald.

DONALD: Would you do it?

Lights dim slightly and then flash on and off as a light thunder rumbles.

RICHARD: *(considers carefully)* Would I try it? Why sure, I suppose I might. I put it down to the power of black magic or mind over matter or the mysterious powers of autosuggestion. *(making up his mind)* Yes, to save my life I would accept a small part of some other person's life if I could get it. In the last resort a dying man will clutch a straw. Right, when I think of it Donald, yes you should try this. Magic sometimes works you know.

DONALD: This is not magic of any kind. But Richard, what I meant was, would you do it for me. Would you give me one or two years of your lifetime just to extend my life a little?

RICHARD: *(horrified)* You're asking me for MY lifetime? Why, if I hadn't had that strange dream about you, Donald, I would think that you were a raving lunatic but, sad to say, I can see and sense that strange powers are at work here and I must be careful. *(slowly, thoughtfully and sadly).* There are strange clouds and some light thunder in the heavens. Somehow I feel that this is serious . . . No Donald, I would not sell you any years of my life.

DONALD: Not even for our friendship's sake?

RICHARD: No Donald, life is the most precious thing in the world. I might give you a year and have only a year to live. This supernatural bargaining is all just confusion and madness. It isn't going to work. I may die myself very soon, who knows?

DONALD: *(looking at the Angel of Life)* How many years have you left? *(Angel of Life holds up nine fingers)* You have nine, I know it. Give me just one of those years or I will die tonight. Perhaps we could spend the next year improving your ranch for your young grandson to take over in eight years time.

RICHARD: Donald, I am too wealthy for that to matter to me. I have quite enough for my grandson to take over. Nothing could persuade me to sell any of my years of life. If you're intent on this strange bargaining you need to find a poorman who might sell you a year or two in return for a better but shorter life and I don't mind helping you to try to find such a person.

DONALD: *(desperately)* Richard, you're my oldest friend. Surely you'll not just turn me down flat. What about six months?

RICHARD: *(agonizing)* I'd like to think that this whole thing is a delusion. I hope it is. But I don't care to take a chance on it. If this is all a ghostly and mysterious bargain and I think it is, I wouldn't give anyone one day of my life for all the gold in the world.

DONALD: *(brokenly)* Richard, I don't blame you. You've been honest with me and I thank you for that. That is the sign of your decency and friendship. I feel better now. I can travel ahead into that great far country where we all must go one day.

RICHARD: *(bowing)* Donald, I must go now to try to help you. There are some poor vagrants who sometimes hide out in the thickets over there. *(he points right-stage)* There's an old lost graveyard half-buried somewhere in that jungle.

DONALD: But why? And why have you been searching those woods in secret these many years?

RICHARD: Many years ago, after I returned from the wars with great bombs ringing in my ears, I could not find my truelove. Donald, you've found yours but I'm still searching. Although rich in some ways I am poor in others. That's another reason why I can't give you any years of my life. I must search on and on for my lost truelove and I have heard rumors that she's been seen in the far woods at times.

Enter the angels *who join the Angel of Life. They dance in the background as Richard sings*

THE CITY'S TOILS AND SNARES
Sung: Moderately and Sadly

VERSE ONE:

$s_1 - l_1$ t_1 l_1 t_1 r_1 $r_1 - r_1$ $t_1 - l_1 - s_1$

My love was as fair as a sunlit day

r_1 m_1 $s_1 - s_1 - s_1$ l_1 s_1

As sweet as a summer song

$t_1 - d$ r $r - r$ r t_1 $r - m$ $m - r$

I dreamed we would dance the bright stars away

$t_1 - l_1$ s_1 m_1 d t_1 l_1

From dusk to day's red dawn

$t_1 - d$ $r - r$ r t_1 r m m r

But visions come from dim ghosts that play

t_1 s_1 m_1 d t_1 l_1

How soon the grand mask fades

s_1 l_1 t_1 $l_1 - t_1 - r_1$ $r_1 - r_1$ t_1 l_1 s_1

For she walked away to the streets of gray

$r_1 - r_1$ $m_1 - s_1$ s_1 l_1 s_1

In the city's toils and shades

VERSE ONE:

My love was as fair as a sunlit day
As sweet as a summer song
I dreamed we would dance the bright stars away
From dusk to day's red dawn
But visions come from dim ghosts that play
How soon the grand mask fades
For she walked away to the streets of gray
In the city's toils and shades.

REFRAIN:

s_1 - l_1 t_1 l_1 - t_1 r_1 r_1 - r_1 t_1 - l_1 s_1

I dreamed we would dance through the sunlit trees

r_1 m_1 s_1 s_1 l_1 s_1

To live by streams and glades

s_1 l_1 t_1 l_1 t_1 - r_1 r_1 t_1 l_1 s_1

But she chose the mean streets, the snares, the webs

r_1 r_1 m_1 - s_1 s_1 l_1 s_1

Of the city's toils and shades

REFRAIN:
I dreamed we would dance through the sunlit trees
To live by streams and glades
But she chose the mean streets, the snares, the webs
Of the city's toils and shades.

VERSE TWO:
For young girls thrill their fluttering hearts
By flittering in this way
Like a fish that jumps into a net
Then flips and swims away
She chose to leave those sunlit trees
To change her name and face
But she lost her way through the streets of gray
In the city's toils and shades.

RICHARD: I know that I am not the only one who has lost a truelove. There are many like me.

DONALD: I'll go and try to find someone like that. Perhaps a poorman would share with me more than a richman.

RICHARD: Donald take heart. There are only two kinds of people in the world - those who've been told they will die soon and those who will die soon but who've not been told. Only cowardice makes us want to live in ignorance. The end result is the same for all.

Donald leaves the stage and Richard remains, prancing up and down in agitation and guilt.

- Curtain -

ACT THREE
BEGGARMAN, THIEF

SCENE ONE: A TRAMP IN A HOBO DEN

The curtain opens on right-stage now revealed as a Skid Row hobo den - an old deserted graveyard in the back hills. This is highlighted with mellow spotlights as a subsection of the previous scene, up to now hidden by bushes.

Jack, a tramp, huddles around an old fire. Right-stage there are a few cans, bottles and pans scattered about. It is a raw evening and Jack is dressed in torn overalls, old shoes and straw hat. His stick and bag are nearby.

Jack takes a small gold-framed photograph from his bag and sets it down to look at it. He nostalgically shakes his head in regret as he looks at his torn clothes and then around the hobo den. He stares into the distance remembering his lost love of long ago, lifts the photo, holds it by his side and looks at it from time to time as he sings.

JACK: On days like this I seem to see my lost love from days gone by.

Jack sings

LADY OF DAYS GONE BY
Sung: Irregular and Romantic

VERSE ONE:

d   r - m   f   d taw_1 l_1 - f_1 - maw_1
When old time songs and sad serenades

f_1 l_1 - d taw_1 l_1 f_1 f_1 - *f_1*
And old time dreams are in   the air

d   r   m   f - d taw_1 - l_1 f_1 - maw_1
There comes a lady dancing alone

f_1 l_1 - d taw_1 - l_1 f_1 f_1 *f_1*
An old-time lady who is fair

f   s - l   taw   f   maw   r - taw_1 - law_1
She dances dreams like wild   melodies

f   s   l   taw   f   s   s   l - l   *taw*
Of old dead loves that long and linger on

d   r   m - f   d taw_1 l_1 - f_1 - maw_1
She brings alive those old   memories

f_1 l_1 d taw_1 l_1 f_1 f_1 - *f_1*
She weaves the scenes of love now gone

REFRAIN:

f s l taw - f maw - r - taw_1 law_1

She is a lady dancing   fair

f s l taw f s s   l - l   *taw*

She is a dream from where sweet memories flow

d r m f d - taw_1 - l_1 - f_1 - maw_1

She comes to dance   mysteriously

f_1 l_1 d taw_1 l_1 f_1 f_1 - *f_1*

Like one I loved long, long ago

VERSE ONE:

When old time songs and sad serenades
And old time dreams are in the air
There comes a lady dancing alone
An old-time lady who is fair
She dances dreams like wild melodies
Of old dead loves that long and linger on
She brings alive those old memories
She weaves the scenes of love now gone.

REFRAIN:

She is a Lady dancing fair
She is a dream from where sweet memories flow
She comes to dance mysteriously
Like one I loved long, long ago.

VERSE TWO:
Her eyes are calm. They linger and love
And flash and glance with living flame
As though she stepped in wonder and awe
From some old golden picture frame
Her hair is thick and flowing like flowers
Like flowers I gave to one - long yesterday
Her friendly voice is like the dear voice
Of one I loved, long gone away.

Enter from right Lorita and Rosaleen as memories from the past. Lights dim and a spotlight plays on the figure of Lorita who dances in and out of the shadows. The figure of Rosaleen sings **The Calm Springtime Snow.**

THE CALM SPRINGTIME SNOW
Sung: Calmly and Reflectively

VERSE ONE:
   d   f   l   s   f   f   m   r   f   r   d
Sweet love, I remember the dear times gone by
f l d^l d^l taw   l   s   f   f   m   f   s
Not once did we dread that our true love would die
   d   f   l   l   s   f   f   m   r   f   r   d
But our love went adrift in the world's too and fro
   f   l - d^l d^l taw l d f m   f s   f
And somehow wept away like a faint springtime snow

REFRAIN:

f r¹ r¹ r¹ taw d¹ r¹ d¹ f s l
The dreams of this world are so mean and so vain
l taw d¹ taw l l s f f-m f s
Lives are ruined in a way that we cannot explain
d f l l s f f m r f r d
But our love was not dead it was just lost we know
f-l d¹ d¹ taw l d f m f s f
And now it's returned like the calm springtime snow

VERSE ONE:
Sweet love, I remember the dear times gone by
Not once did we dread that our true love would die
But our love went adrift in the world's too and fro
And somehow wept away like a faint springtime snow.

REFRAIN:
The dreams of this world are so mean and so vain
Lives are ruined in a way that we cannot explain
But our love was not dead it was just lost we know
And now it's returned like the calm springtime snow.

Lorita waves her hands at the landscape.

VERSE TWO:
For meadows need sunshine as well as the rain
If life is to flourish and spring up again
We have now met once more and wherever we go
Love will always be fresh like the calm springtime snow.

Lorita and Rosaleen disappear.

JACK: *(in agony)* Come back Rosaleen. *(looking around and startled)* Where? Where have you gone? *(shaking his head sadly)* Ah dear, it was just a dream like many a dream. This place is haunted by spirits of the past.

Enter the Angel of Life and the angels unseen by Jack who sings verses three and four of LADY OF DAYS GONE BY

VERSE THREE:
Men crave for many a bauble and more
For treasure, wisdom, strength or skill
But you have in your eyes a flame
That burns with longings cool and still
As though your dreams had all come true to life
I yearned to share your joy right from the start
The joy that made your favorite ones
Go daily dancing around your heart.

VERSE FOUR:
Perhaps I envied you your joy
That was the yearning I called love
There are souls who are fed on happiness
Like flowers in the secret arts of grace
Perhaps I saw that still content
Calm and unhurried in your eyes like doves
Perhaps I envied you, your joy
That was the yearning I called love.

*The angels dance among the graves and nearby the tramp to the tune of **LADY OF DAYS GONE BY**. They weave imaginary spells above their heads and are unseen by the hobo. However, as the song and dance come to an end, the hobo appears to be slightly disoriented and shivers as though having a bad dream. Although he cannot see the angels, he seems to sense something strange in the air. The mood becomes even more mystical after the brief song is finished. Jack remains preoccupied with his memories and oblivious to the entrance of Donald.*

Enter Donald following the Angel of Life and her angel friends.

DONALD: It was sad about Richard my old friend.

Donald Sings
DOES PAIN REMAIN
Sung: Slow and Sad

VERSE ONE:

f   s   l - l   f   d   taw$_1$ l$_1$
When friend betrays and hinders
taw$_1$ d   f   f - f   f
And we forgive the friend
   s   l   s   l   taw   d^1 d^1 l
Why still does memory linger
  d^1 taw   r   m   r   d
And pain remain in mind?
   l   d^1 d^1 l   d^1 taw - l
With heart burned to a cinder
   l   f - f   r - r   taw
We leave old loves behind
   f   s   l - l   f   d   taw$_1$ l$_1$
Ah, why does memory linger
taw$_1$ d   f - f   f   f
And pain remain in mind?

VERSE ONE:
When friend betrays and hinders
And we forgive the friend
Why still does memory linger
And pain remain in mind?
With heart burned to a cinder
We leave old loves behind
Ah, why does memory linger
And pain remain in mind?

VERSE TWO:
When lands flame up like tinder
New peaceful fields we find
So why does memory linger?
Must pain remain in mind?
When points that Mighty Finger
Across the tide of time
Even there, does memory linger?
Does pain remain in mind?

ANGEL OF LIFE: Donald, a hint of the other world has invaded these deserted tombs since we began to move among them. Some of the hobos have left already. This poor tramp sitting here alone cannot see me or my angels but perhaps he senses our presence.

DONALD: *(walking about distractedly)* Yes, although invisible, you have created a sinister mood here today that may help me to be believed. But am I really hoping to bargain with this poor wretch? Have I become a mere beggar of time?

ANGEL OF LIFE: No, Donald, you cannot be seen as a beggar.

DONALD: My life is too short to waste time being laughed at. So let me make a deal with Jack the hobo, if I can. Leave me alone with him for a little while.

ANGEL OF LIFE: *(sighing)* Very well Donald, we will leave you, unseen but watching.

The Angel of Life and her angel friends leave stage right.

Donald approaches the fire.

DONALD: *(rubbing hands)* It's cold.

Jack nods.

DONALD: *(continuing)* And it's miserable here.

Hobo nods suspiciously, looking Donald up and down.

DONALD: *(uncertainly)* Maybe I can help you a little?

JACK: I'm in the business of taking any help I can get.

DONALD: *(continuing to rub his hands and lowering his voice)* Perhaps you'd let me give you some money.

JACK: *(shivering)* Money, well why not give it to me right now. Why talk of it? I had a funny feeling earlier that something strange would happen today. *(looks up at the heavens)* See what I mean, a real richman, a wealthy farmer *(looks Donald up and down)* has come and is just handing out money.

DONALD: Wait, let me explain.

But Jack continues talking.

JACK: Do you want me to kill your wife or your boss or your father? These are the three most common victims. No! Keep your money. I don't do those things. I'm mostly honest, that's why I'm poor. *(looks around and shudders)*

DONALD: I've been warned by the Angel of Life, a messenger of the Great Master, that my natural years have run out unless I can find a person to sell me some part of his life. Don't misunderstand, I don't want anyone to kill anyone. I just want to buy a little lifetime from someone. I'm dying and I need to buy time – a few years.

JACK: *(slowly)* Buy some of my lifetime? What exactly do you mean?

DONALD: *(gently)* I wish to buy just a little time from you.

Jack is fascinated, thinking, listening carefully, shuddering slightly as he seems to sense but not see the presence of the Angel of Life lurking nearby.

JACK: *(slowly)* You mean that I make a deal with you so that I give you time out of my life and you give me money. And you live longer and I die sooner. Is that it?

DONALD: Well . . yes . . that is . . you die a little sooner but you live in more comfort and ease while you're alive. You sell only as much of your life that you are willing to give up.

JACK: But I have acres of ease. That's why I opted out of the rat-race to take life easy. I wouldn't like to cut my lifetime short for any amount of money. We get all types here in old Skid Row - people who think we're for sale, body and soul but we're not. We just want to be left in peace.

Long ago my truelove left me and I lost everything. The only thing I want now is for her to come back.

DONALD: But you're not comfortable, well fed or happy!

JACK: *(with some antagonism)* No sir, it's not comfortable here but it's quiet and relaxed most of the time. You think money can buy anything, don't you?

DONALD: Think of it this way, you would be giving life to someone else in return for your own independence.

JACK: *(puzzled but intrigued)* It's a weird deal. I dunno. It must be black magic or something. *(thinking and nodding)*

DONALD: *(desperately)* I'm just trying to help both of us, that's all. Let me prove my goodwill. Here, take some money please with no strings attached, just as a gift. This will show you that I mean you no harm.

Donald takes out a few dollars

JACK: *(lying down and turning his head away)* Get out of here.

DONALD: Take this gift of a few dollars. No exchange needed.

JACK: *(squatting by the old fire and lowering his head)* Keep your black magic money. Leave me to get on with my life. *(sitting down, picking up a small stone and tossing it casually at Donald)* Beat it, mister. Neither you nor your money are wanted here. Can't you take a hint?

Jack, with half-closed eyes, casually throws another small stone at Donald. It is clear that Jack is not trying to hit Donald with the stone but is merely trying to frighten him.

DONALD: *(with just a little resentment)* One day you may regret this. I did offer you an honest bargain . . *(pauses)* even if a strange one. Your life cannot be at peace my friend, sleeping in the cold. You're shortening your life by living in poverty. Life is a graveyard while you live and death is a graveyard when you die. See, this is a graveyard not a mansion or a cottage. A little help might have made life better for you.

JACK: *(bitterly)* Get out. In this life we always regret what we do, no matter what. So leave me alone.

(aside) A wise man in some small ways but aren't we all wise in some small and trivial ways. He's rich but mad as a hatter in all important things.

No . . not crazy exactly but with only a few days left to live - terribly desperate I'd say - at his wit's end.

Yes and dabbling in black arts to try to save his life. *(shakes his head in distrust)*

Jack hurries off stage right and is followed by Donald but all the angels remain.

- Curtain -

ACT THREE
BEGGARMAN, THIEF

SCENE TWO: LATER IN THE DEN
Same as the previous scene but later in the day.

Enter the Angel of Life and the angels. *They stand around the periphery of the stage dancing to the music of* **THE CALLING ANGEL SONG.**

Enter Lorita, *a widow and her daughter* **Rosaleen,** *carrying bags and wearing shawls and long skirts. They join in the dancing. One at a time the angels merge into the trees and leave. The Angel of Life, Lorita and Rosaleen continue to dance center-stage in around the hobo den. The music slowly dies away and they stop dancing, center, in the dim light.*

LORITA: Who is this strange lady in white, dancing among the springtime flowers?

Lorita approaches the Angel of Life and smiles a friendly greeting. Then Rosaleen and Lorita draw their shawls more tightly around their shoulders as a light wind stirs.

ROSALEEN: *(looking around in fear)* It's cool today.

LORITA: More than cool, it's eerie too! *(she shivers again)* It was on such a day as this that the great bombs blew apart my world and yours. This reminds me of the coldness of war.

Images of marching soldiers cross the stage behind the singer. Drums tap out and flutes play the tune in martial beat, e.g., on screen, backdrop or with actual actors.

Lorita sings

SWEETHEARTS LOST IN WAR
Sung: Slow and Stately

VERSE ONE:

l - fe   r   m   fe   s   m   l   s m - r r   de   r
O where are the rains that fell on winters past and gone?

l l r^1 t r^1 de^1 l   t   s   m   m   fe
Where are the storms that wrecked good ships from dusk

s   l
to dawn?

l l r^1 t - r^1 de^1 l   t   s   m - m   fe   s   l
Where are the hails and sleets that froze down from the sky?

s - m - r   m   fe   s - m   l   s   m   r   r   *r*
Ah, where are the sweethearts of the good times gone by?

VERSE ONE:

O where are the rains that fell on winters past and gone?
Where are the storms that wrecked good ships from dusk
to dawn?
Where are the hails and sleets that froze down from
the sky?
Ah, where are the sweethearts of the good times gone by?

VERSE TWO:

Where are the battle drums that led so fierce and proud?
Where are the raging guns that fired so red and loud?
Where are the dread young men who marched to fight
and die?
Ah, where are the sweethearts of the good times gone by?

LORITA: *(to the Angel of Life in a tone of awe)* Who are you?

ANGEL OF LIFE: I am a messenger of new life.

LORITA: *(drawing back)* I feared that you were not of this world.

ANGEL OF LIFE: I am of this world and of the World of Everlasting Tomorrows. I bring the two great worlds together for I am the Angel of Life whom the Great One sends to call the dead and dying ones over the Great River of Parting. My fellow dancers are angels who escort the souls of the dead across that eternal river.

LORITA AND ROSALEEN: *(drawing back in terror)* Not us, surely not now? *(shaking their heads)* Not so soon!

They hold up their hands defensively.

ANGEL OF LIFE: *(gravely)* Not yet, ladies but one day I must call on all. *(changing her tone to a milder but still accusing key)*

Now that I have told you who I am, let me tell you who you are. You say you are dancers or hostesses or girls having a good time but you are none of these. You are just petty thieves who steal. One of your easiest victims is the rich and tired farmer coming home from the market after he has sold his livestock - like Donald who often fell for your hardluck stories.

Lorita and Rosaleen appear humiliated but puzzled and sadly shrug their shoulders at each other.

ROSALEEN: Perhaps my mother begged a little, so what?

ANGEL OF LIFE: That does not concern me. My business is with greater matters. Donald is coming here tonight and I must see to it that you do not think him crazy or getting old in mind, that you do not try to humor or cheat him. He has a serious bargain to present. He wants to buy some of your lifetime and you must decide whether your answer is truly 'yes' or 'no'.

ROSALEEN: *(with enthusiasm)* Why mother, Donald is a rich farmer. What a chance to become rich even if the price is to die a little sooner. Why, we're down and out - what have we to lose except a little time - never a problem for us before now.

LORITA: *(avariciously)* Wealth at last within our grasp. *(to Angel of Life)* Tell us Angel of Life about the other life. Is my late husband Carl there, Rosaleen's father? Will my daughter and I meet some of our dear old friends long passed away in the wars and will we recognize each other? Will we have our sense of identity and our memories? Is there a good home for us there?

ANGEL OF LIFE: *(coolly)* I cannot tell you of your eternal destiny. There are good lands and badlands in the hills beyond.

LORITA: But you said yourself that we were only petty thieves and beggars. Surely that wouldn't be enough to send us to a bad place. Tell us now if that is the case. We have a right to know.

ROSALEEN: Yes, so that we can . . so that we could change our way of life in time - if necessary. You have a duty to tell us?

ANGEL OF LIFE: *(angrily)* I have no such duty! You have plenty of preachers and philosophers. I am not here to judge or instruct or guide. I am here only to call home the soul of Donald the farmer in obedience to the Great Master of Life. Your behavior and your conscience is a matter for yourselves. I must stand aside now for Donald is here.

Angel of Life steps into the shadows and exits. Enter Donald.

DONALD: *(talking to himself)* I have searched for poormen all around the den but they've all said no. Jack has gone. *(shakes his head)* To where? *(stops - looks at the others, solemn but pleased)* Why it's Lorita and Rosaleen waiting. It's just like oldtimes.

LORITA: Donald, I'm so sorry. We heard . . the Angel of Life has told us about your life . . you're not well.

ROSALEEN: *(with genuine concern)* So soon after your marriage. It's tragic.

DONALD: So the messenger has spoken to you? *(they affirm)* That is just as well for I could never have explained it. *(shakes his head)* I wouldn't believe it myself. I would have thought it was all a dream. I'm afraid that it's not a dream. It is true. I've been sick in times past but never before have I felt the chill of death.

LORITA: I've always heard that strange happenings take place sometimes before a death such as banshees, apparitions, strange animals appearing and so on.

DONALD: It's sadly real. It's as though someone was pointing a loaded gun at my brain, right between the eyes and her finger tightening upon the trigger. I hope that you two old friends can help me to escape. You both need money?

LORITA: *(evasively)* Perhaps. *(doubtfully)* Well, we're pretty sure we can help you.

DONALD: If you help me to extend my life a little . . .

LORITA: Well, let's talk about it. I know I've probably only a few years left myself. Perhaps Rosaleen, my daughter, would be willing to make an investment with you for a large sum. I'm sure she has many years left.

ROSALEEN: Who me? I thought that you would be the one. You've had a full life.

LORITA: Me? But I've only a few years left.

ROSALEEN: *(scornfully to Lorita)* But you've lived all of your years, mother, not shortened your life in any way by any weird deal. I dread the unknown and the Angel would tell us nothing. We don't know how many years we would have left. *(dubiously and slowly)*

Lorita gives a "hush" negative hand signal to Rosaleen and turns to Donald.

LORITA: *(smiling)* Donald you should have married my daughter Rosaleen. She's a little jealous, perhaps. There's so much inheritance, *(she numbers off on her fingers)* the big farm, the pigs, the poultry, the crops, the wood, the sheep, the equipment, the horses, the cows, so much wealth still to be left to your wife. Maybe you could raise a half million if you just sold some livestock. You could still leave the farm to your wife later.

DONALD: *(looking into the distant hills and nodding slowly)* Perhaps.

LORITA: See, Rosaleen, half a million is a lot of money. What do you say?

ROSALEEN: *(as though stunned and doubtful)* I don't know. Maybe the money should all go to your wife, Donald. After all, she's expecting it. She did marry an older man no doubt to inherit your farm and wealth. Didn't she?

DONALD: *(quietly)* No, Rosaleen. That is not true. My wife's own father owned a big farm, too. She has never been poor.

LORITA: *(outraged)* Never poor? Hah! *(quickly)* So what? *(slowly and outraged)* The more you have, the more you want. Since when has money been a cure for greed?

DONALD: *(with sorrow)* But Lorita, you don't understand. Marcella has been a good wife to me.

LORITA: *(with raised eyebrows and snapping her head back, with hands on hips)* Indeed!

ROSALEEN: *(with light sarcasm)* Oh yes, I'm sure she has been a great wife to you, Donald. I would behave myself too for a short while to inherit so much. Who wouldn't? And yet here you are trying to cheat her out of her early inheritance. I'm not sure that it's quite fair of you to extend your life in this way. Will you make your wife wait until she is middle aged to get her just reward? No doubt she's hoping to marry a younger man one day. Now that she is a young and pretty and a wealthy widow, she could marry anyone. But when she becomes older and gray and fat she will only be able to marry someone who looks for money.

LORITA: *(anxiously)* Rosaleen let Donald's wife look out for herself. What's that to us? Don't tell me that you have changed your mind and that you're not going to make a deal with Donald to give him some lifetime even for a half million or more?

ROSALEEN: Mother, if it's so good a bargain, why don't you make a pact yourself. I'm not sure, Donald. I don't want to die one day sooner than I have to.

Donald looks from one to the other, puzzled and concerned.

LORITA: I'm not sure either, Donald.

DONALD: *(rubbing his forehead and eyes reflectfully and walking up and down restlessly)* Not sure? I need to know! Tell me . . yes or no?

Lorita and Rosaleen look doubtful and troubled then shake their heads slowly.

DONALD: *(sadly and dejectedly but as one making the best of a bad situation)*
Well, perhaps you're right. Maybe it's time for me to go to the Hills of Everlasting Tomorrows and to let my Marcella have her freedom. She's been a good wife; she has a right to everything. *(with quiet perceptiveness)*
I miss my old true friends all killed in war. Surely one of them would have helped me.
Donald sings:

FRIENDS OF LONG AGO
Sung: *Slowly and Sadly*

VERSE ONE:

d r   m f m   f   s   f   r taw₁ *d*   d   *d - d*
I remember the good friends of so long, long ago
f s l *taw* l taw *dˡ taw* l   taw   l   taw *dˡ*
All our talk and our laughter and love's too and fro
  d   r m f   m f   s   f   m   f   m
Though it is now many years since those friends went
 f s
away
  d r   m f   m   f   s   f   r taw₁ *d*   d   *d - d*
Deep inside in my heart I can still see them today
d r   m   f m   f   s f   m   f   m f   s
The kind neighbors now parted that we used to know
d r m   f   m   f   s   f   r taw₁ *d*   *d - d*
Oh,   where are the good friends of   long ago?

VERSE ONE:
I remember the good friends of so long, long ago
All our talk and our laughter and love's too and fro
Though it is now many years since those friends went away
Deep inside in my heart I can still see them today
The kind neighbors now parted that we used to know
Oh, where are the good friends of long ago?

REFRAIN:
Oh where are the dear friends who have gone on before?
Do they live in the shades of a happier shore?
For we cannot bring back all the loved ones now gone
So we weep and we wonder, does their life go on?
Will we all walk together in a far land one day?
Or have they just gone with the wind far away?
Will we too soon be gone with the wind far away?

VERSE TWO:
They say that time heals - that is the greatest of lies
We may sometimes forget but the pain never dies
When companions have left, when dear friends
have gone
There is always a sorrow that must linger on
O the sickness and madness of war have no end
There is a part of your life that will die with your friend.

ANGEL OF LIFE: *(to Donald)* Surely now you must be resigned at last Donald and at least somewhat in peace. Let us go now to where springtime flowers are always blooming and there is no more weeping.

DONALD: *slowly and thoughtfully he sings:*

THE FLYING SONG

VERSE ONE:

d^1 l f f - m f   r taw$_1$ d
I will fly along the song-bird's sky
  d r m f   s l - taw s d^1
Swooping around, a jovial flyer
  d^1 d^1 l f f - m f r taw$_1$ d
To all I know below, I'll call goodbye.
  d r m f - l   r s m f
While the small people cling - I will fly.
  d f m f s l - taw d^1
I'll smile to see their creeping ways
  r^1 d^1 d^1 l f s l - d^1 taw l - s
As I climb and rise and circle up higher
d^1 l f f m f r - taw$_1$ d
I will swing and sing of winging days
  d r - m f l r s m f
While above all things I, I will fly.

VERSE ONE:
 I will fly along the song-bird's sky
Swooping around, a jovial flyer
To all I know below, I'll call goodbye.
While the small people cling - I will fly.
I'll smile to see their creeping ways
As I climb and rise and circle up higher
I will swing and sing of winging days
While above all things I, I will fly.

VERSE TWO:
High over clouds and rains I'll fly
Far above the fear and lying
A free-bird strong in song and mirth, I'll cry.
From the sad sigh of earth - I will fly
Up where the air is new and true
Through a glad sky where no-one is pining or dying
I will glide in flight across the blue
But above all things I, I will fly.

DONALD: Before I go, let me say goodbye to my wife.

ANGEL OF LIFE: *(spreading her hands in a gesture of resignation but bowing respectfully)* You may do so, for death is a terrible parting but do not be long.

All leave the stage right.

- Curtain -

ACT FOUR
OLD FRIENDS

SCENE ONE: BACK AT THE FARM
Scene: ***Enter Donald,*** *sits on an old log, chin resting on his hand, his face shows some pain and sorrow as he stares at the distant trees and hills. Donald stands up and paces back and forward slowly for a few seconds. He is brave, not panicked or afraid but rather seems resigned and sad.*

Enter Marcella *running and alarmed. She stops, surprised, when she sees Donald. She puts her hand to her mouth as though taken aback.*

MARCELLA: Oh thank goodness you're all right, Donald. I was afraid. A strange apparition, someone who seemed to be more than human, appeared before me and told me to bid you goodbye . . that your time was short. She told me where to find you. It must have been an illusion.

(questioningly) You are all right, Donald?

DONALD: *(gently)* No, not quite. I fear I am near death.

MARCELLA: *(interrupting)* But you're not dying, Donald? Are you ill? Let me get a doctor for you. No, let me get you to hospital. But you're fit and strong. You'll be all right, Donald.

DONALD: *(sadly and firmly)* My dear, it's time for us to part. I have tried so hard to extend my life but it's no use.

MARCELLA: *(puzzled)* To extend your life but I don't understand, Donald. You've not been ill . . .

DONALD: No, but early today I received a warning from the Angel of Life that my time had come to leave this world. Then I was given a chance to extend my life.

MARCELLA: *(mystified)* Then I don't understand, Donald. Why did you not take this chance?

DONALD: *(taking Marcella's hands)* I could not, my love. I tried so hard but failed to find someone who would make a deal with me to give me a few years of their life in return for whatever I could give them.

Marcella shakes her head in confusion and disbelief.

Marcella, I could find no one of all I knew, neither richman, poorman, beggar or thief who would make a pact to give me some of their lifetime in return for any of my wealth.

Marcella continues to shake her head.

I was so sad. It bore me down with fear.

MARCELLA: Why didn't you tell me, I'll gladly give you one half of my remaining years. Perhaps, who knows, I might have about 40 years still left. That will be 20 more years each for both of us to share together. Isn't this fair?

DONALD: *(shocked)* Marcella, I can't ask you to do this.

MARCELLA: But don't you see that life would not be good for me without you.

DONALD: Look Marcella, you're young. You need all the years of your life. You need a chance to marry a younger man and I'm getting old.

MARCELLA: *(laughs)* But Donald, you weren't the only one who asked me to marry. I've already rejected my younger suitors. How silly men are! Did you think that I couldn't have chosen a younger man? What a horrible thought that I should be a wealthy widow. *(laughs)* Please try to see it. You were my only choice.

Enter the Angel of Life followed by her angels.

ANGEL OF LIFE: *(in the background unheard by Donald or Marcella)* Donald, this is an acceptable bargain. You will recover and live.

Donald appears to regain his strength. Marcella and Donald dance center stage.

All remain in position.

- Curtain -

ACT FOUR
OLD FRIENDS

SCENE TWO: OLD LOVES REVIVED - FINALE
Scene: Donald and Marcella are in much the same places with minor variations on the positioning of the props.

DONALD: *(to Marcella)* I've invited all our friends to celebrate our new life together.

Enter Richard

RICHARD: Congratulations Donald and Marcella. It's difficult to get the better of Time and yet you've managed it, Donald, with the help of Marcella.

Time is a dreary detective who dogs our footsteps and destroys our peace of mind.

Time is the runner who cheats in the race and despite his cheating - wins.

We lose the race and are amazed. We cannot believe that we have lost.

But how Time cheats and deceives us!

Time, if you listen closely to his

footsteps, ticks away slowly in seconds, craftily and cunningly he pretends to go slowly.

But if you take your attention away from Time's slow steps, to look at your work or leisure, Time jumps up. He becomes another person and cheats you.

He flies above you, runs unexpectedly around you or takes shortcuts when your back is turned even for a moment.

He leaps over ravines, vaults over creeks and trees and robs you in every way to get there before you. Then the race is over before you could possibly expect it.

You have lost and Time has won. Yes, Time cheats us and deceives us to destroy.

But a young wife brings good years of life and joy.

Ah and here comes my long lost love, Lorita, who left me many years ago.

Enter Lorita, *sings last verse of* ***SWEETHEARTS LOST IN WAR.***

VERSE ONE:

 l - fe r m fe s m l sm - r r de r
Where are the battle drums that led so fierce and proud?
 l l r^1 t r^1 de^1 l t s m m fe s l
Where are the raging guns that fired so red and loud
 l l r^1 t - r^1 de^1 l t s m - m fe
Where are the dread young men who marched to fight
 s l
and die?
 s - m - r m fe s - m l s m r r *r*
Ah, where are the sweethearts of the good times gone by?

Where are the battle drums that led so fierce and proud?
Where are the raging guns that fired so red and loud?
Where are the dread young men who marched to fight
and die?
Ah, where are the sweethearts of the good times
gone by?

Richard is overjoyed.

RICHARD: Lorita, my lost love, you were my only friend and one truelove. This song was for me. It seems to echo in my memory like a song I heard in a dream. The wars deranged my mind and I thought you left me.

LORITA: Oh, what a loss not only of a friend but of the years as well.

Enter Jack, *bowing to others, sings* *LADY OF DAYS GONE* - *Verse 2.*

VERSE ONE:

  d   r - m   f   d   taw$_1$ l$_1$ - f$_1$ - maw$_1$
Her eyes are calm. They linger and love

  f$_1$ l$_1$ - d   taw$_1$ l$_1$ f$_1$ f$_1$ -*f$_1$*
And flash and glance with living flame

  d   r   m   f - d taw$_1$ - l$_1$ f$_1$ - maw$_1$
As though she stepped in wonder and awe

  f$_1$ l$_1$ - d   taw$_1$ - l$_1$ f$_1$ f$_1$ *f$_1$*
From some old golden picture frame

  f   s - l taw   f   maw r - taw$_1$ - law$_1$
Her hair is thick and flowing like flowers

  f   s   l taw f s   s   l - l *taw*
Like flowers I gave to one - long yesterday

  d   r m - f   d taw$_1$ l$_1$ - f$_1$ - maw$_1$
Her friendly voice is like the dear voice

  f$_1$ l$_1$ d taw$_1$ l$_1$ f$_1$ f$_1$ -*f$_1$*
Of one I loved, long gone away

Her eyes are calm. They linger and love
And flash and glance with living flame
As though she stepped in wonder and awe
From some old golden picture frame
Her hair is thick and flowing like flowers
Like flowers I gave to one - long yesterday
Her friendly voice is like the dear voice
Of one I loved, long gone away

Enter Rosaleen

ROSALEEN: Jack, so you're still alive? After all these years we meet at Donald's invitation and I didn't even know that Donald knew you.

*Sings to Jack, **THE CALM SPRINGTIME SNOW** - Verse 1.*

Sung: Calmly and Reflectively

VERSE ONE:

　　d　f　l　s　f　f　m　r　f　r　d
Sweet love, I remember the dear times gone by
　f l　d^1　d^1　taw　l　s　f　f　m　f　s
Not once did we dread that our true love would die
　d　f　l　l　s　f　f　m　r　f　r　d
But our love went adrift in the world's too and fro
　f　l - d^1　d^1　taw l　d　f　m　f　s　f
And somehow wept away like a faint springtime snow

Sweet love, I remember the dear times gone by
Not once did we dread that our true love would die
But our love went adrift in the world's too and fro
And somehow wept away like the faint springtime snow

Jack joins Rosaleen. They hold hands.

Enter the Angel of Life and all the dancers now dressed as Queens of Spring. All dance.

ANGEL OF LIFE: One day your souls will be carried across that great river where you will dwell with the Great Master of Life.

They sing FRIENDS OF LONG AGO
Sung: Slowly and Sadly

VERSE ONE:

d r   m f m   f   s   f   r   taw₁   d   d   d - d
I remember the good friends of so   long, long ago

f s   l   *taw*   l taw d^l *taw*   l   taw   l   taw d^l
All our talk and our laughter and love's too and fro

  d   r m f   m f   s   f   m   f   m
Though it is now many years since those friends went

 f s
away

  d r   m f   m   f   s   f   r taw₁   d   d   d - d
Deep inside in my heart I can still see them today

d r   m   f m   f   s f   m   f   m   f   s
The kind neighbors now parted that we used to know

d r m   f   m f   s   f   r taw₁   d   d - d
Oh,   where are the good friends of   long ago?

VERSE ONE: (RICHARD)
I remember the good friends of so long, long ago
All our talk and our laughter and love's too and fro
Though it is now many years since those friends went away
Deep inside in my heart I can still see them today
The kind neighbors now parted that we used to know
Oh, where are the good friends of long ago?

REFRAIN: (DONALD, MARCELLA, LORITA, ROSALEEN)
Oh where are the dear friends who have gone on before?
Do they live in the shades of a happier shore?
For we cannot bring back all the loved ones now gone
So we weep and we wonder, does their life go on?
Will we all walk together in a far land one day?
Or have they just gone with the wind far away?
Will we too soon be gone with the wind far away?

VERSE TWO: (JACK)
They say that time heals - that is the greatest of lies
We may sometimes forget but the pain never dies
When companions have left, when dear friends have gone
There is always a sorrow that must linger on
O the sickness and madness of war have no end
There is a part of your life that will die with your friend

LORITA: *(to Donald and Marcella)* You're most fortunate to live and cross over together. Many make this journey of life and death alone.

Lorita and Rosaleen link up again with their lost loves Richard and Jack. They hold hands.

ANGEL OF LIFE: Farewell, Donald and Marcella. One day we will meet again. Until then be filled with the joy of springtime. And now I put the cloak of forgetfulness between you all and my presence.

She swings a cloak between them. Lights dim and focus on Donald and Marcella who dance center as the rest of the company, forming into a background dance, call out a farewell to Donald and Marcella as the lights fade.

As the Angel of Life and her angels leave stage there is a flashback to the original Act One, Scene One and Donald is discovered by Marcella sitting on a log. The rest of the company are in the shadows at this point. Donald had been sleeping but is now awake.

Lights.

*The rest of the company are revealed as Donald and Marcella sing, **OLD FRIENDS** with backing from the Company and bowing and hand shaking.*

Sung: Slowly with Feeling

VERSE ONE:

d   m   m - m   r   m   s   s

When old friends meet and greet, ah then

d^1 l   s   l d^1 l   s - s

The old bread springs to joyful grain

d - d   m   m m - r   m   s   *l*

And the wine is always strong and sweet

s - s   m   r   d - d

When old friends greet and meet

s - s d^1 d^1 - t t   l   l

Good days will always fleet and flee

d^1 s   l - l - s   f - m m r - r

And old times change with memory

d - d - m   m m   r   m   s   *l*

But old friends are real and whole and true

s - s   m   r   d - d

When old friends meet anew

d - r   m   r   d

Old friends are few

d   r   m   m - m - r   *d*

(So) Old friends are always new.

WHEN OLD FRIENDS MEET

VERSE ONE:

When old friends meet and greet, ah then
The dry bread springs to joyful grain
And the wine is always strong and sweet
When dear friends greet and meet
Good days will always fleet and flee
And past times change with memory
But old friends are real and whole and true
When good friends meet anew
Good friends are few
(So) Old friends are always new.

VERSE TWO:

Old hands are warm to grip and greet
And hearts will give a stronger beat
Dim eyes will see more clearly then
When old friends meet again
Good days will always fleet and flee
And past times change in memory
But good friends are real and whole and true
When dear friends meet anew
Old friends are few
(So) Old friends are always new

- Curtain -
END OF PLAYSCRIPT

APPENDIX
FIVE FINGER EXERCISE
Simple Instructions on How to Play the Tunes

Music is presented in the form of tonic sol-fa. Tonic sol-fa is the written form of music for both beginners and virtuosos – those who do not need guidance on timing, arrangements or chords – those who need only the basic tune.

1.   Hitting the Right Note
2.   White Keys - Stick-On Labels
3.   Black Keys - Stick-On Labels
4.   Getting the Timing Right
5.   Summary

HITTING THE RIGHT NOTE

C is the white note just to the left of the two black notes side by side. Find Middle C on your keyboard. A register is the level of a set of tonic sol-fa. Here is the location of Middle C on a standard three register keyboard. The white note in the exact middle of any keyboard is Middle C (in staff) and Doh (in tonic sol-fa).

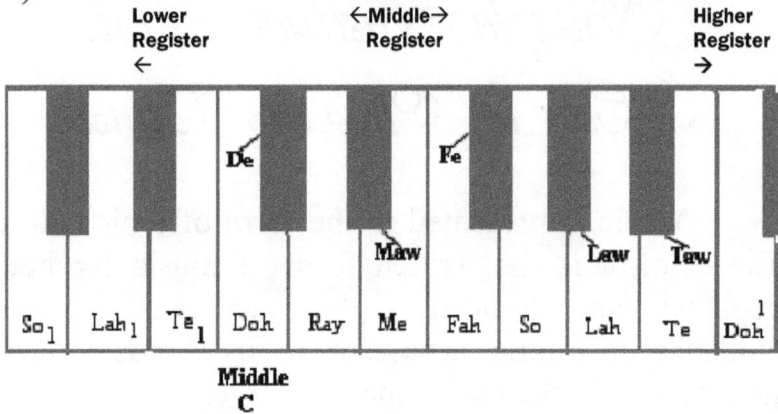

Lower Register ←			←Middle→ Register							Higher Register →
			De			Fe				
					Maw			Law	Taw	
So$_1$	Lah$_1$	Te$_1$	Doh	Ray	Me	Fah	So	Lah	Te	Doh¹

Middle
C

The tunes in this songbook can all be played on these three middle registers. Larger keyboards may have additional higher or lower registers but these will not be needed for the simple basic tunes in this book.

C is always Doh and going up from Middle C is the central set of tonic sol-fa:

Doh, Ray, Me, Fah, Soh, Lah, Te.

The next note is also a C and is the Doh higher than Central Doh. This starts off the next register of tonic sol-fa notes.

The Middle Set of tonic sol-fa have no subscript or superscript: d, r, m, f, s, l, t.

The Lower Register (set of tonic sol-fa) have subscripts as follows: $d_1, r_1, m_1, f_1, s_1, l_1, t_1$.

The Higher Register (set of tonic sol-fa) have superscripts as follows: $d^1, r^1, m^1, f^1, s^1, l^1, t^1$.
Here is a complete set of labels, for the white and black keys, to stick onto your central basic keyboard.

WHITE KEYS: STICK-ON LABELS FOR YOUR KEYBOARD

LOWER REGISTER	Doh_1	Ray_1	Me_1	Fah_1	Soh_1	Lah_1	Te_1
MIDDLE REGISTER	Doh	Ray	Me	Fah	Soh	Lah	Te
HIGHER REGISTER	Doh^1	Ray^1	Me^1	Fah^1	Soh^1	Lah^1	Te^1

WHITE STICK-ON NOTE INSTRUCTIONS

These are to be stuck on to your keyboard to show you which notes to play as you follow the Tonic Sol-fa music set out in each song.

1. The seven white notes with subscripts (lower register) lead up to Middle C.

APPENDIX

2. Middle C starts off the middle register of seven white notes that have neither subscripts nor superscript.

3. The seven white notes with superscripts (higher register) follows on after the middle register.

Only the last three white notes of the lower register and the first white note of the higher register are shown with the middle register in the keyboard diagram.

THE BLACK KEYS

The black keys in each register are as follows:
de, maw, fe, law, taw.

The five black keys in the lower register
have subscripts
The five black keys in the middle register
have no subscripts or superscripts
The five black keys in the higher register
have superscripts.

Here are the three sets of labels to stick onto the black notes on your keyboard.

LOWER REGISTER	De_1	Maw_1	Fe_1	Law_1	Taw_1
MIDDLE REGISTER	De	Maw	Fe	Law	Taw
HIGHER REGISTER	De^1	Maw^1	Fe^1	Law^1	Taw^1

GETTING THE TIMING RIGHT

(1)   Notes that are grouped together have hyphens between them - to show that they are played together. (eg: d - f - l). This does not mean that such notes are speeded up, only that they are joined together.

(2)   Notes that are to be held longer than average are written in italics - that is to say they are sloped to the right (eg: *d* or *s*).

(3)   Try to follow the hints at the head of each tune (eg: slow and simple or fast and warlike).Keep a steady and regular beat whether the tune is fast or slow (eg: tap your foot or get a friend to tap out an even measured beat).

SUMMARY

Below is a diagram of all three registers - Lower, Middle and Higher. Of course, on many keyboards and pianos there are more than these three registers but these keys are all that you will need to play the simple tunes in this songbook

Lower Register   **Middle Register**   **Higher Register**

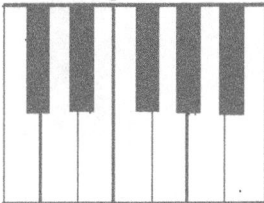

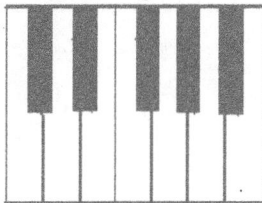

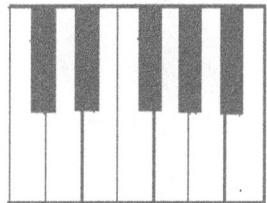

← Middle C →

← Subscripts →   **← Superscripts →**

APPENDIX

BRIEF INSTRUCTIONS

1. Cut out the squares and stick them on to the black and white keys.

2. Hit the notes asked for in the tonic sol-fa tunes, trying to hear each melody as a whole and keeping a steady beat.

**Key to
Tonic Sol-fa
Notes**
D = doh
R = ray
M = me
F = fah
S = soh
L = lah
T = te

WHITE KEYS: STICK-ON LABELS
FOR YOUR KEYBOARD

LOWER REGISTER	Doh_1	Ray_1	Me_1	Fah_1	Soh_1	Lah_1	Te_1
MIDDLE REGISTER	Doh	Ray	Me	Fah	Soh	Lah	Te
HIGHER REGISTER	Doh^1	Ray^1	Me^1	Fah^1	Soh^1	Lah^1	Te^1

BLACK KEYS: STICK-ON LABELS
FOR YOUR KEYBOARD

LOWER REGISTER	De_1	Maw_1	Fe_1	Law_1	Taw_1
MIDDLE REGISTER	De	Maw	Fe	Law	Taw
HIGHER REGISTER	De^1	Maw^1	Fe^1	Law^1	Taw^1

APPENDIX

HOW TO IMPROVE YOUR SINGING

In singing these songs there are seven main aspects of singing to check out and practice towards perfection. (There are also several more subtle, complex and minor aspects which only a real-life music teacher could explain. Each aspect of singing calls for separate exercises as well as putting all six together.

1. Voice Quality
Largely a given, quality can be developed by practice, healthy diet and deep breathing.

2. Diction
Concentrate on sharp clear pronunciation to achieve understanding on the part of the listener. Aim for sounds that most people with standard English, not accents, will understand.

3. Projection
Throw out the voice until all the audience can hear it. Every word must always reach the listener.

4. Phrasing
A phrase is a group of words and notes that are grouped together. Watch how the sounds and words hang together and change the combinations until it sounds right to you in your opinion. What is right for one singer may not be right for another.

5. Feeling

Try to imagine how the sender of the message would feel and think. Develop a dramatic empathy, a oneness with the message of the song so that it comes over as genuine.

6. Rhythm

Keep an even beat or a creative subtly uneven one. Tap your foot on the ground or follow a drummer, or hand claps (see also the section on timing).

7. True Notes

Make sure that the note you play is the right one. Listen to a self-tape and compare your notes with those sung by a friend or played on a keyboard or other instrument. Sometimes it helps to close your eyes and listen well.

8. Find a Teacher

If you can, find a good singing teacher with top credentials or at least get a musical friend to critique you.

THE END